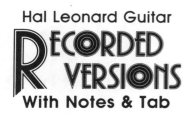

Hal Leonard Guitar

RECORDED VERSIONS

With Notes & Tab

D1594850

U2

Distributed in the U.S.A. and Canada by

HAL LEONARD PUBLISHING CORPORATION

Distributed in the United Kingdom by
MUSIC SALES LTD.

Distributed in all other territories by
IMP International Music Publications

THE BEST OF

Hal Leonard Guitar
RECORDED VERSIONS
With Notes & Tab

U2

Transcribed by Andy Aledort

In order to provide a complete transcription of the album, we've included both guitar and bass parts for each song. The guitar parts are in the first section of the book, following the Notation Guide. The bass parts are in the last section of the book.

CONTENTS

THE BEST OF

NOTATION GUIDE

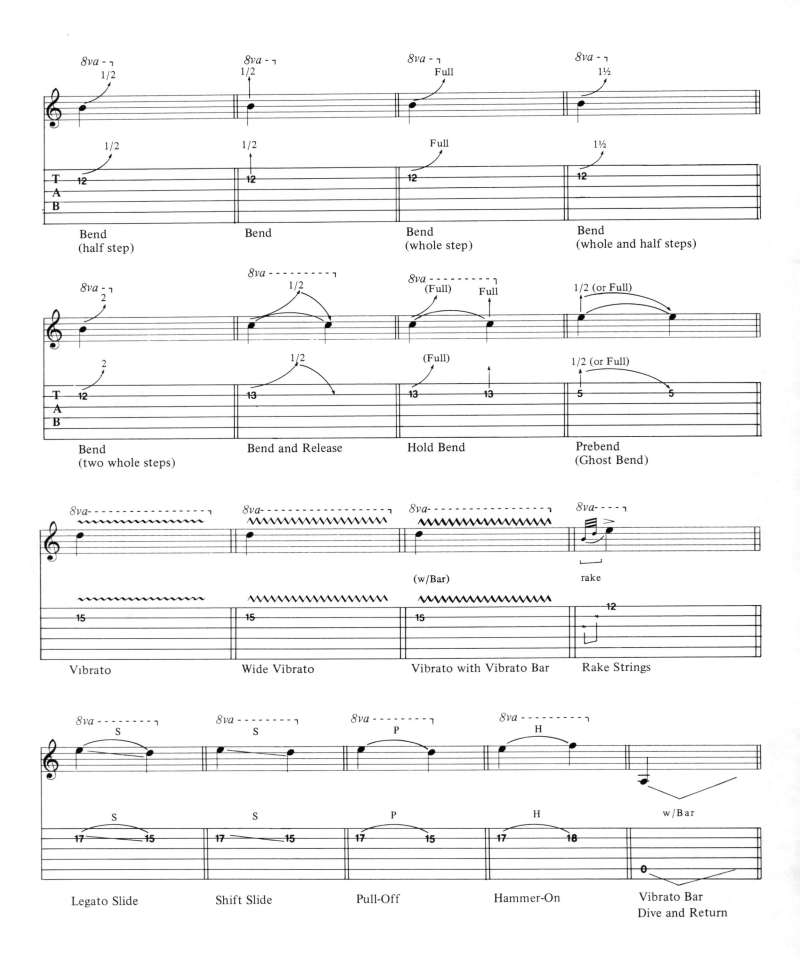

Vibrato Bar Scooping   Ghost Note   Articulated Bend and Release   Artificial Harmonic (with pick) (Overtone of 5th generated)

Pure Artificial Harmonic (octave)   Open Harmonic   Tap Artificial Harmonic   Tap-On Technique

Bend and Tap-On Technique   Percussive Tone (Muffled) (Finger mute)   Heavy Muting (P.M.) (Palm Mute)   Slight Bend (Microtone)

Staccato (shote notes)   Choppy Phrasing (extreme staccato)   Pick Scrapes   Tremolo Picking

Unison Bend   Muting (distinct pitches)   Trill

BAD

Words by BONO
Music by U2

2nd Verse
Repeat Riff A *(2 times)* & Rhy. Fig. 1 *(till next verse)*

If I____ could throw this life - less life - line_ to the_ wind,____ leave_ this

heart of clay, ____ see you walk,_ walk a - way_ in - to the_

____ night._____ And through the____ rain,_____ in - to the_

Repeat Rhy. Fig. 1

____ half_ light,_ and through the____ flame. _____

If I ____ could, through my - self,_ set your spir - it free, _ I'd lead your

heart a - way_ s - see you break,_ break_ a - way_____ in - to the__

____ light_____ and to the day._____

7

If I could,__ you know I would,__ if I could,__ I __ would let it go.__

Rhy. Fig. 2

Repeat Rhy. Fig. 2 *(till next fig.)*

This des - per - a - tion,__ dis - lo -

ca - tion,__ sep - a - ra - tion,__ con - dem - na - tion, rev - e -

D.S. al Coda

la - tion, in temp - ta - tion, i - so - la - tion, des - o - la - tion, let it go

Coda

Begin fade

__ sleep - ing, oh no,__ oh no.

Fade out

GLORIA

Words by BONO
Music by U2

*Chord names derived from bass figure.

I WILL FOLLOW

Moderately Uptempo Rock ♩.= 154

Words by BONO
Music by U2

Intro
1st time—Solo gtr.
2nd time—Drums enter
3rd time—Bass enters
Rhy. Fig. 1

*E Mixolydian (E, F♯, G♯, A, B, C♯, D)
†Chords derived from bass figure.

20

Repeat Rhy. Fig.1, 2 times (2nd time use 4th ending)

2nd Verse

_ tries hard_ to be a man,_ his moth - er takes_ him by his hand_ (if) he

stops to think,_ he starts to cry, _ oh why?_

Chorus

If you walk a - way, walk a - way, walk a - way, walk a - way,_

Repeat Rhy. Fig. 1 *(2 times)*

Chorus

Rhy. Fill 1

*Slide past fretboard.

NEW YEARS DAY

Words by BONO
Music by U2

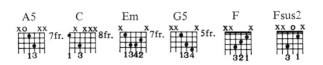

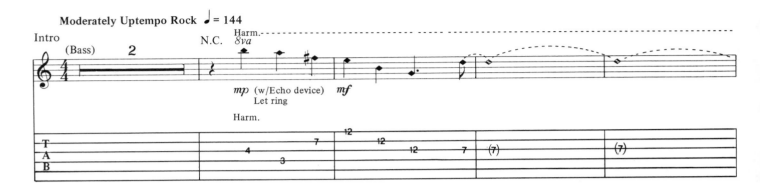

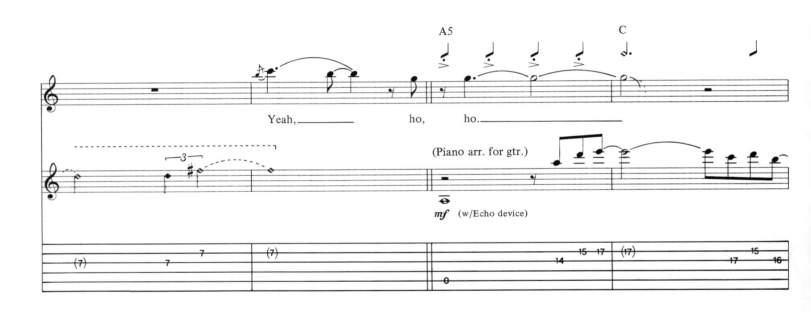

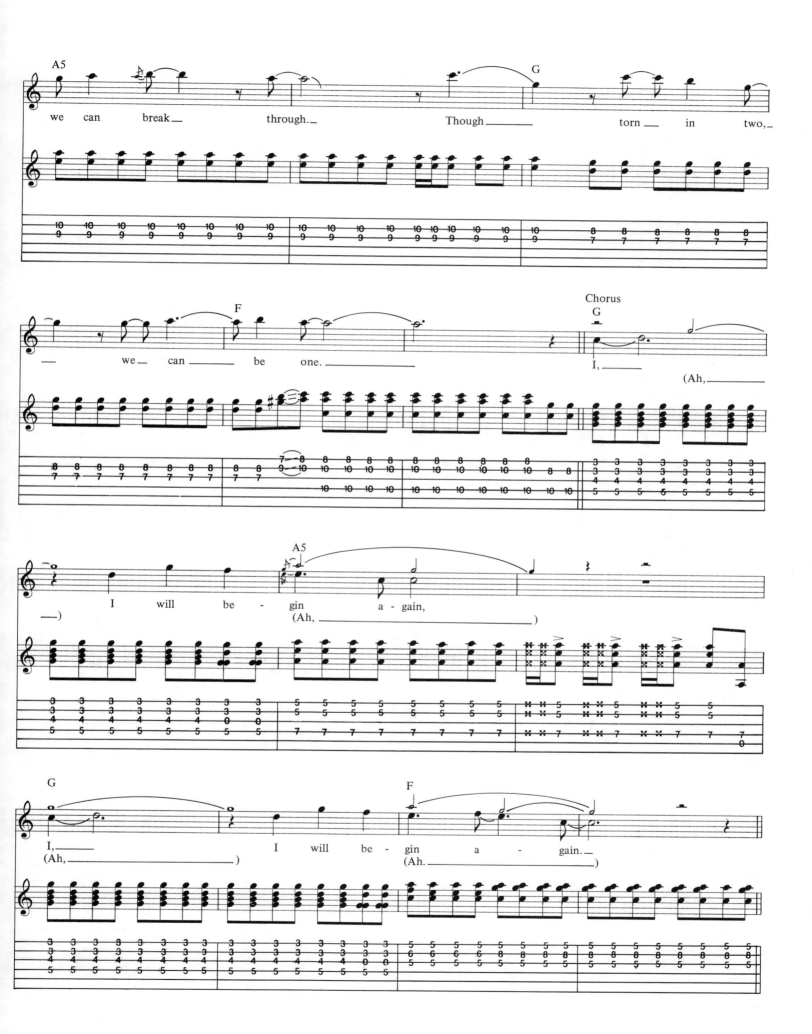

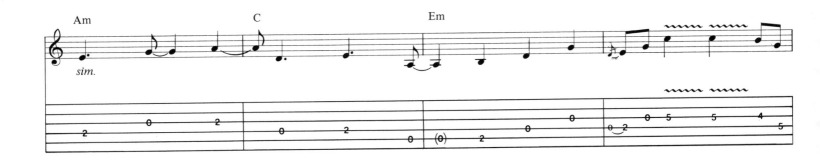

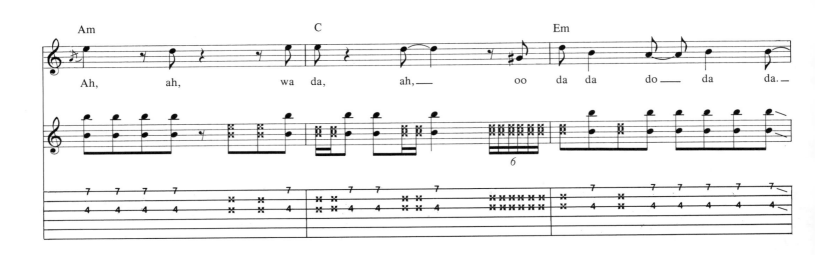

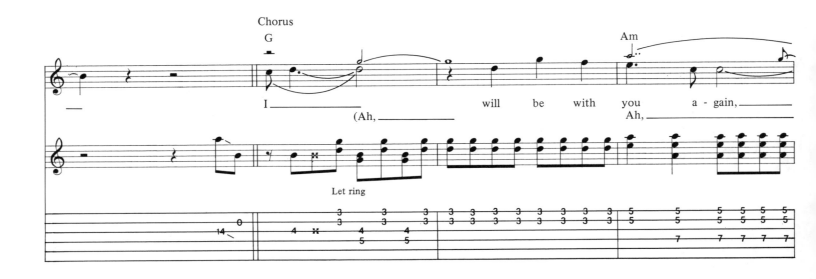

34

OCTOBER

Words by BONO
Music by U2

PRIDE
(IN THE NAME OF LOVE)

Words by BONO
Music by U2

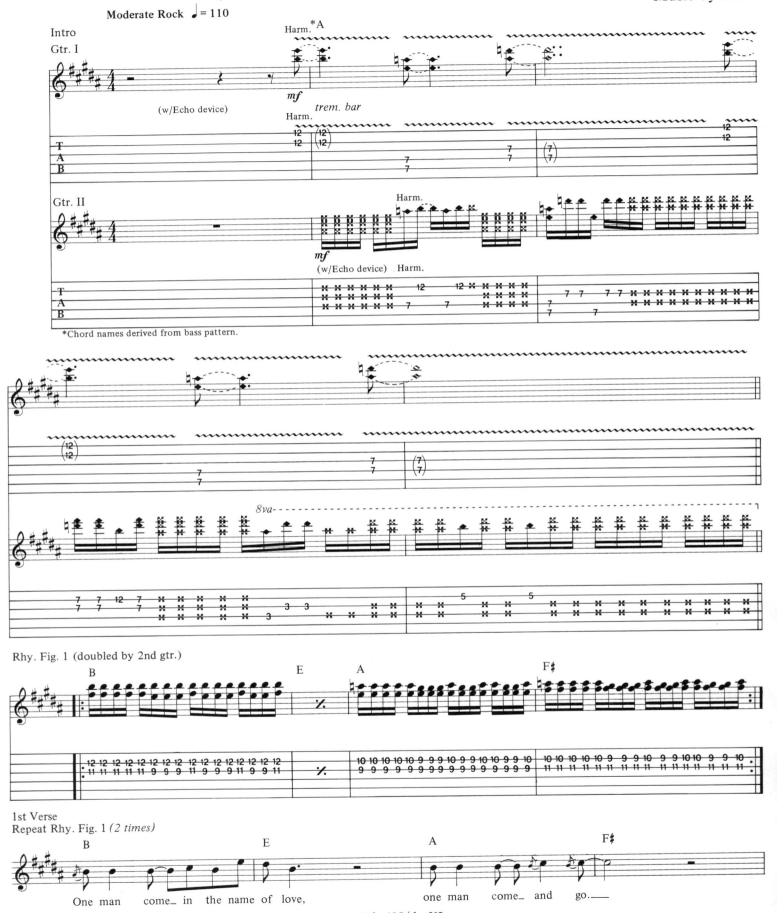

*Chord names derived from bass pattern.

One man come_ in the name of love, one man come_ and go.—

41

SUNDAY BLOODY SUNDAY

Words by BONO
Music by U2

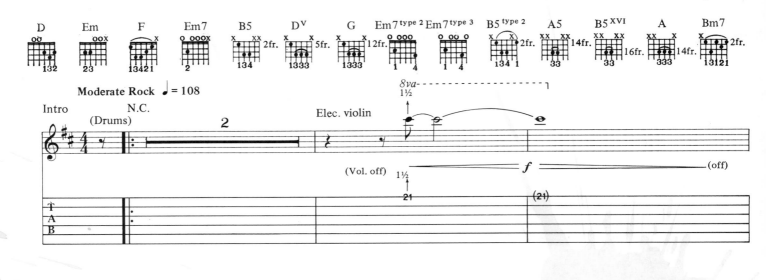

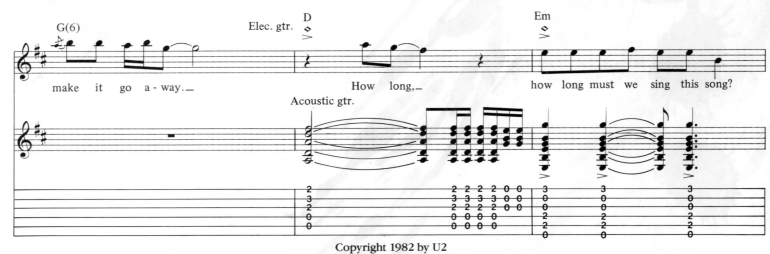

How, long,— how long?_____ 'Cause to-
Ah!

night
Ah. _____ we can be as one,— to - night! Ah,— ah. _____

Elec. gtr. (doubled by
12 stg. acoustic)

Harm. *(15ma)*   Harm. *(15ma)*

Harm. *(15ma)*

Harm.   Harm.   Harm.

2nd, 3rd Verses

2. Bro - ken bot - tles un - der chil - dren's feet,—
3. And the bat - tle's just be - gun,—

*1st time only

*Chord names derived from bass pattern.

SURRENDER

Words by BONO
Music by U2

54

58

*Past fretboard; sounds E

Sur - ren - der.
Sur - ren - der.

Fade out

A SORT OF HOMECOMING

Words by BONO
Music by U2

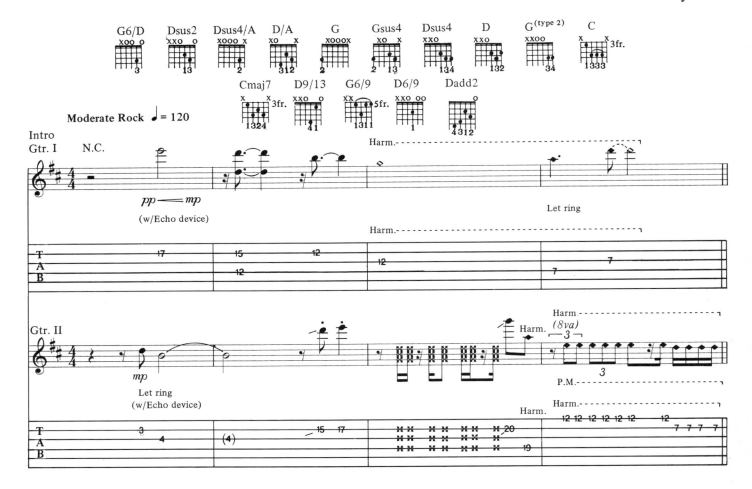

1st Verse (Gtr. II continues ad lib sound effects w/echo*)
Rhy. Fig. 1

*Such as sliding up & down neck, strumming muted stg., etc.

know it's time_ to go,___ through the sleet and driv - ing_ snow,_ a - cross the fields___

_ of mourn -ing (to a) light's in _ the dis - tance. And you

hun - ger for_ the time,_ time to heal,_ de - sire _ time_ and your

earth moves_ be - neath _ your own dream _____ land - scape_____

*low stgs. only
†high stgs. only

Fill 1

65

there   so high___ (land),   I'll be there___   to - night,___   to -

night.

O com - a   way, I   sing___ I   say,   um   ha,   o com - a   way   o   say.___   The wind___ will   crack___

3rd Verse
w/Rhy. Fig. 1

__   in   win - ter - time,___ this   bomb   blast   light - ning   waltz.   No   spo - ken   words,___

w/Rhy. Fig. 2 (2 times) & Fill 5

__   just   a   scream,_____   yeah._____   Oh _____

w/Rhy. Fig. 3

oh. _____   to - night,_____   we'll build a___ bridge___ a -

w/Rhy. Fig. 3A

cross   the   sea   and   land.___   See   the   sky,___   the   burn - ing   rain___   she___

Fill 5

THE UNFORGETTABLE FIRE

Words by BONO
Music by U2

*Hit drumsticks together in time.

74

Fill 3 (Strings arr. for gtr.)

75

*Low stgs. only
†High stgs. only

GLORIA

Words by BONO
Music by U2

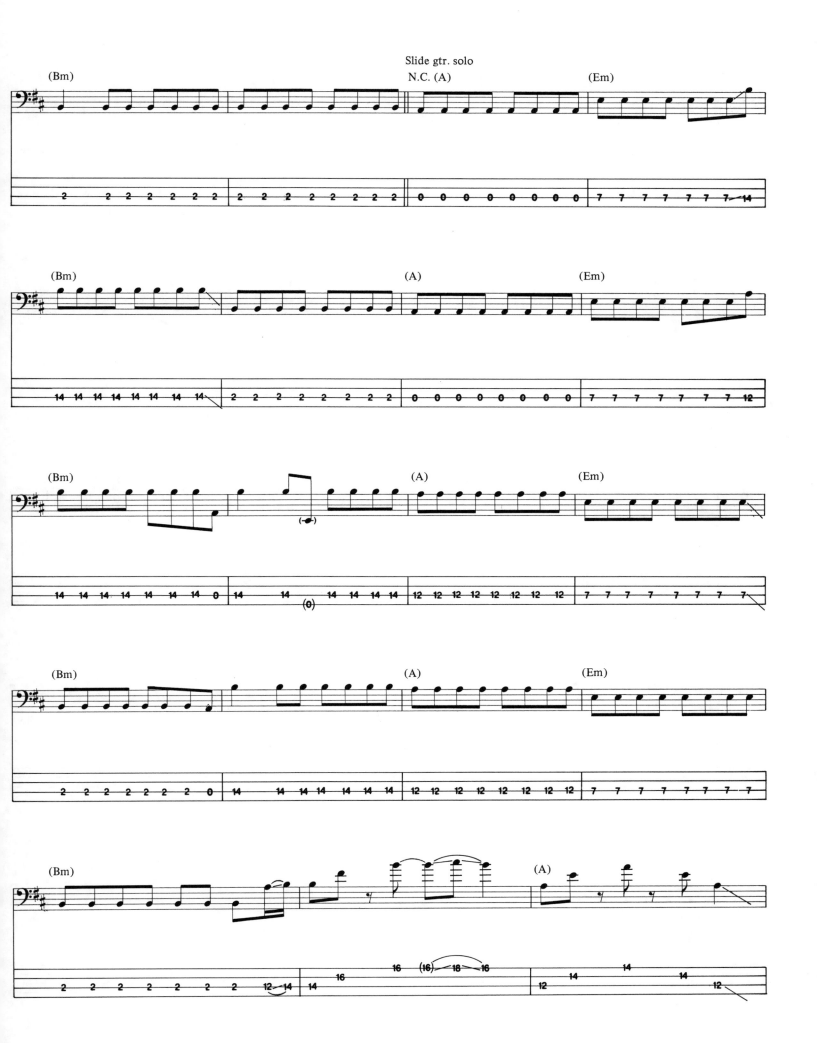

*Snap pizzicato ("snap" stg. against fretboard)

89

BAD

Words by BONO
Music by U2

...I'm not sleep - ing,__ etc.

...let it go_____ etc.

I'm not__ sleep - ing etc.

95

I WILL FOLLOW

Words by BONO
Music by U2

I was on the out - side, *etc.*

*E Mixolydian (E, F♯, G♯, A, B, C♯, D)   †Chords derived from bass figure.

I was on the in-

side, *etc.*

If you walk a-way, walk a-way, *etc.*

walk a - way, walk a - way, *etc.*

NEW YEARS DAY

Words by BONO
Music by U2

OCTOBER

Words by BONO
Music by U2

PRIDE
(IN THE NAME OF LOVE)

Words by BONO
Music by U2

3rd Verse

Early morning, April four, etc.

In the name

Chorus

of love etc.

Play 3 times and fade

112

SUNDAY BLOODY SUNDAY

Words by BONO
Music by U2

114

A SORT OF HOMECOMING

Words by BONO
Music by U2

And you know it's time— to go, — etc.

...heart   beats   so   slow, *etc.*

THE UNFORGETTABLE FIRE

Words by BONO
Music by U2

*Snap pizzicato ("snap" stg. against fretboard).

SURRENDER

Words by BONO
Music by U2

Esus4

Sa -

2nd Verse E

die said she could-n't work— out, *etc.*

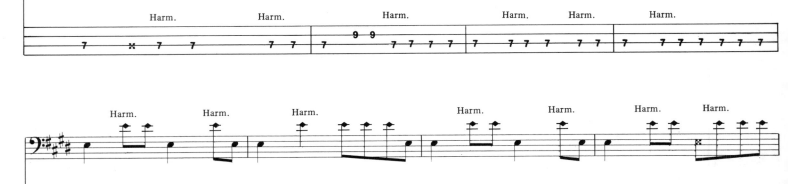

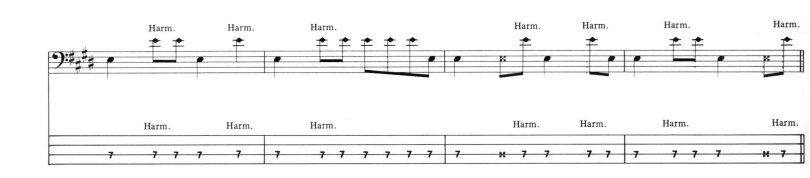

3rd Verse
E

Oh, ___ the cit-y's a - fire,___

etc.

E

Oh_____ etc.

Chorus N.C. (Dsus2)

(Em7)

(Dsus2)

(Em7)   (Em7)   *Play 3 times and fade*